Celebrating
Creative Gifts

feminine coloring pages
with original artwork by Cherie Burbach

Celebrating Creative Gifts

coloring pages

Celebrating Creative Gifts
coloring pages

Bonjour
Publishing

CELEBRATING CREATIVE GIFTS

Printed in the United States of America

Also by Cherie Burbach

Nonfiction

Art and Faith: Mixed Media Art With a Faith-Filled Message

Prayer Warrior Journal

100 Simple Ways to Have More Friends

Glass Sculptures: How to Make Beautiful Sculptures for the Garden Using Vases, Bowls, and Other Glass Pieces

…and more

Poetry

Poiema

Angel Toughness

My Soul Is From a Different Place

Father's Eyes

The Difference Now

A New Dish

New and Selected Poems

Yes, You

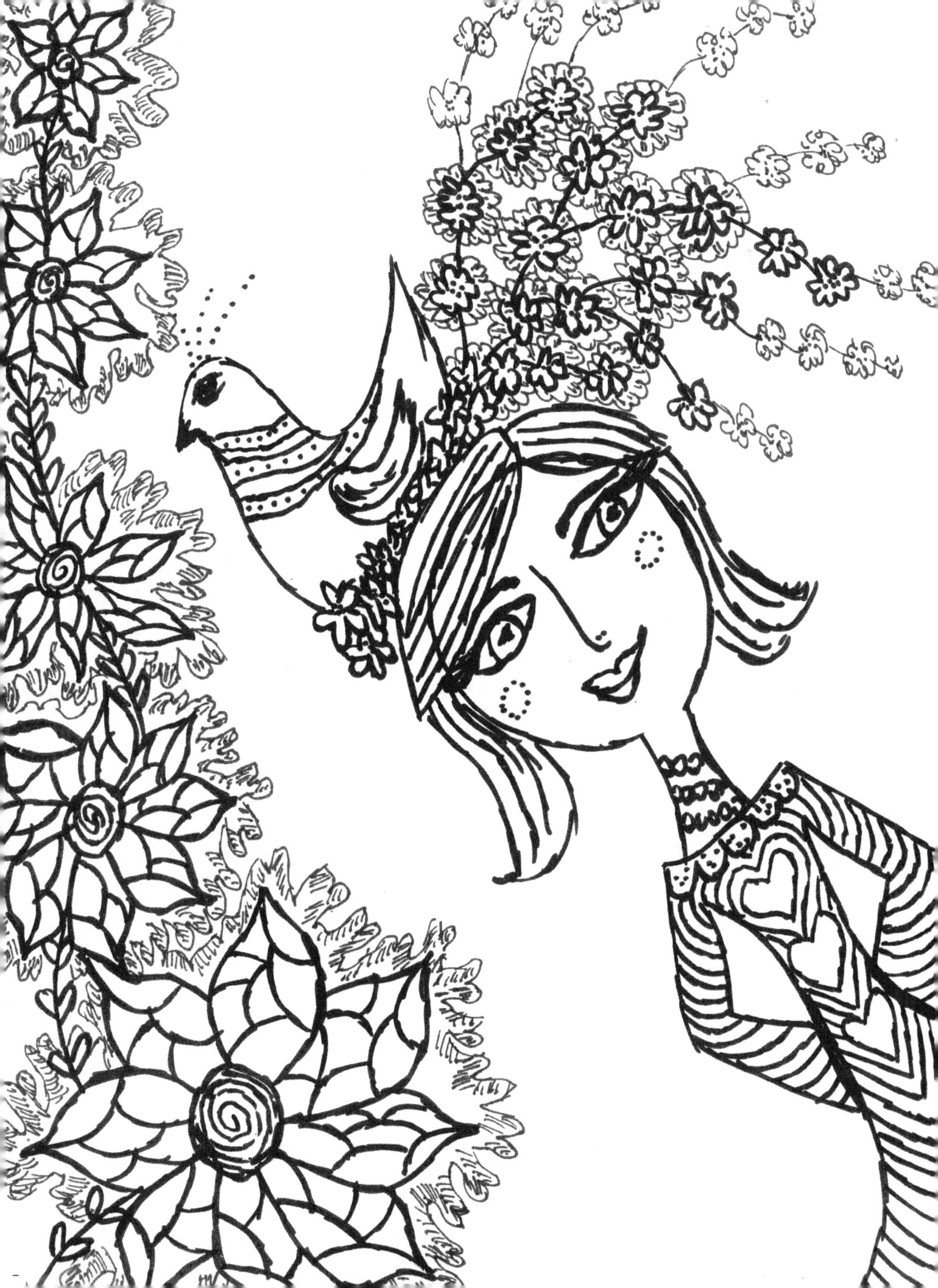

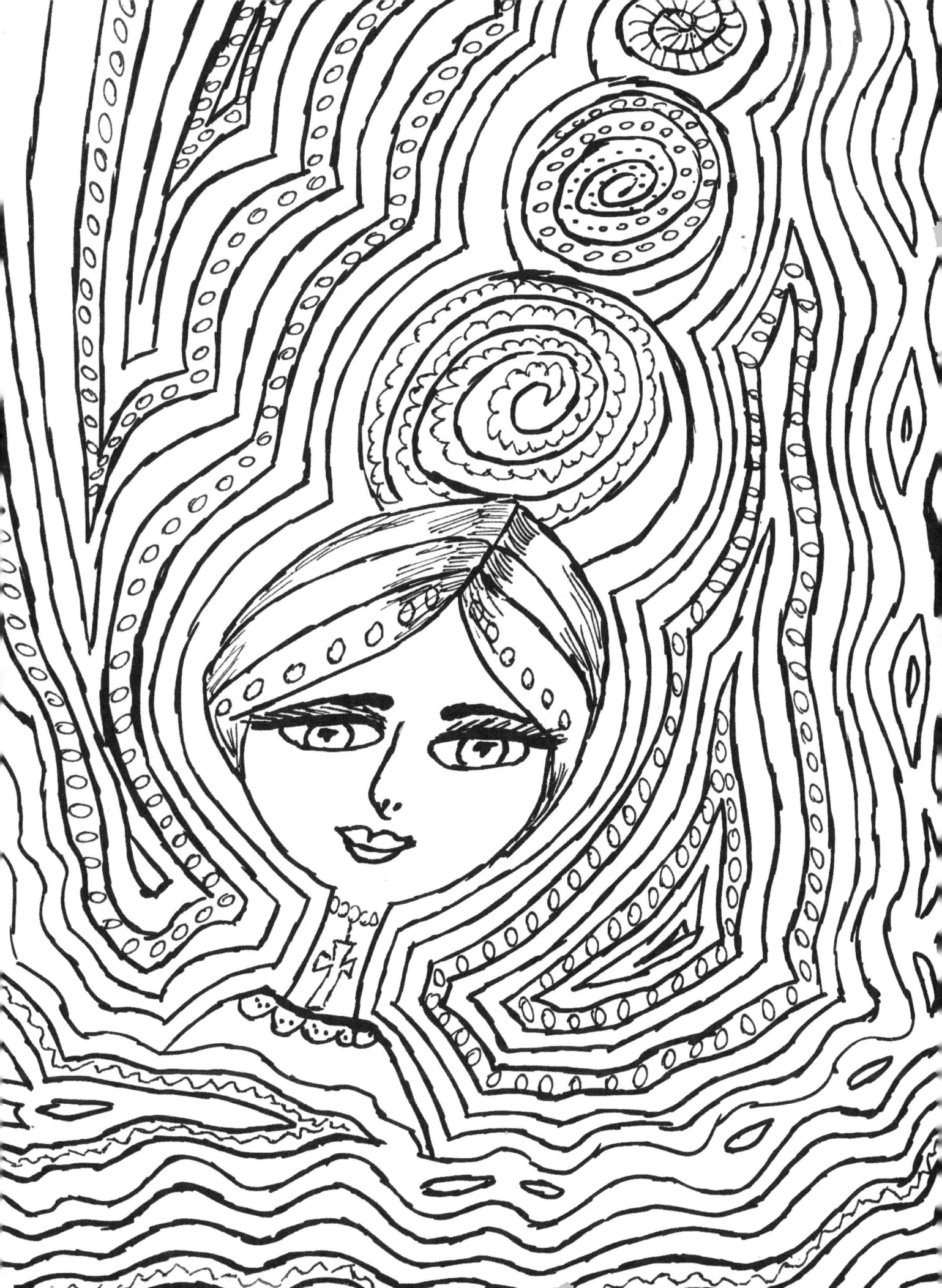

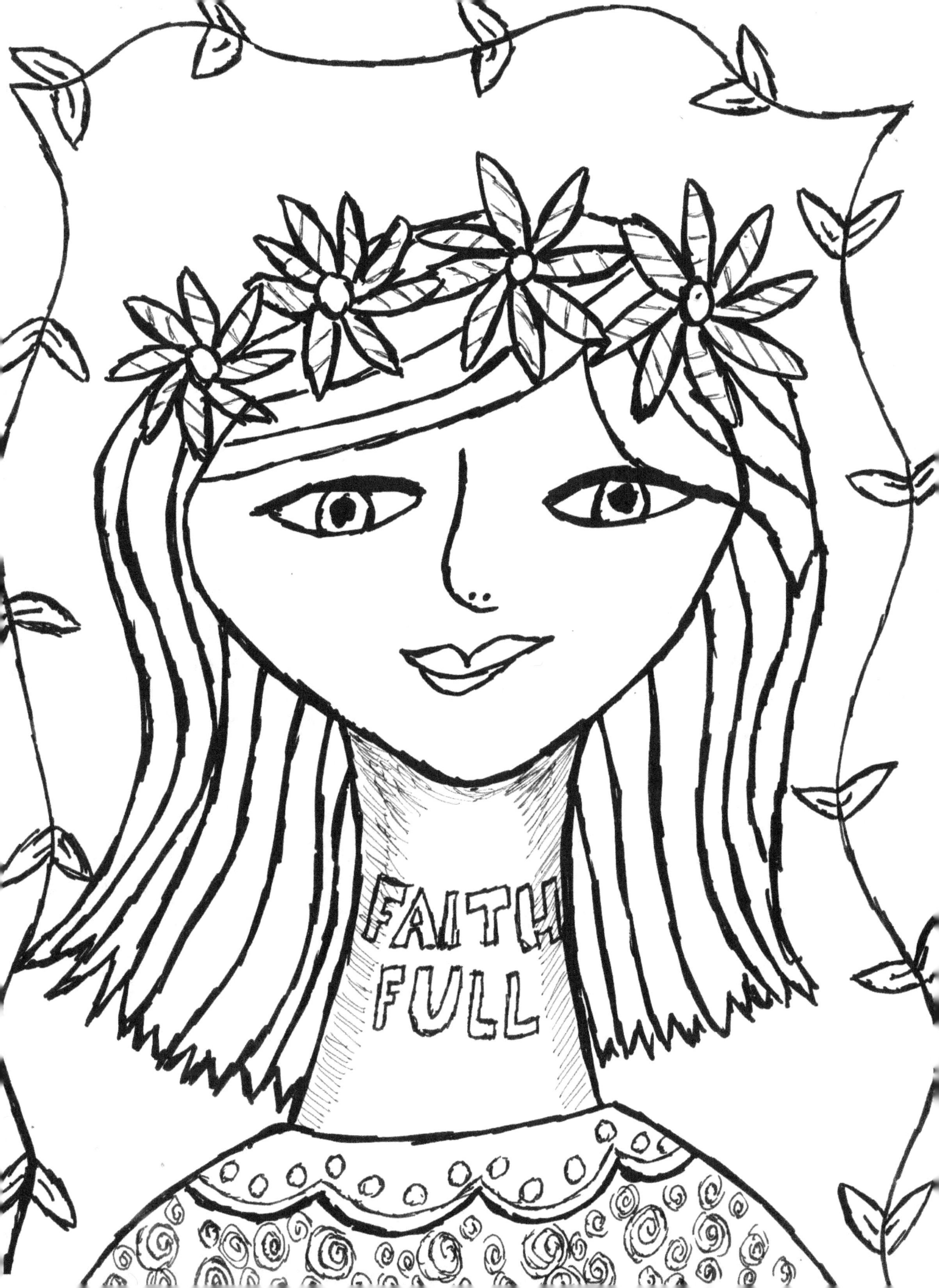

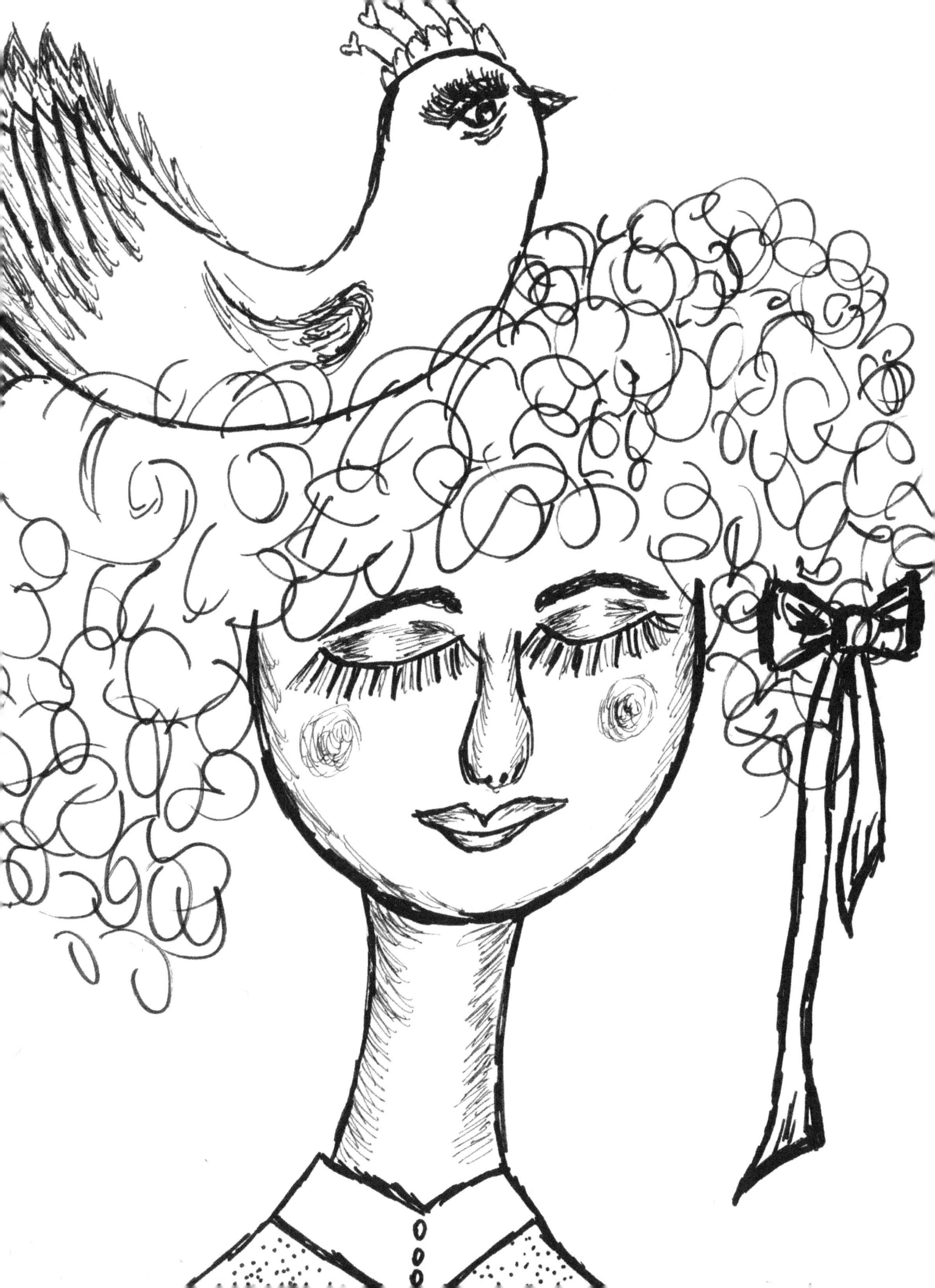

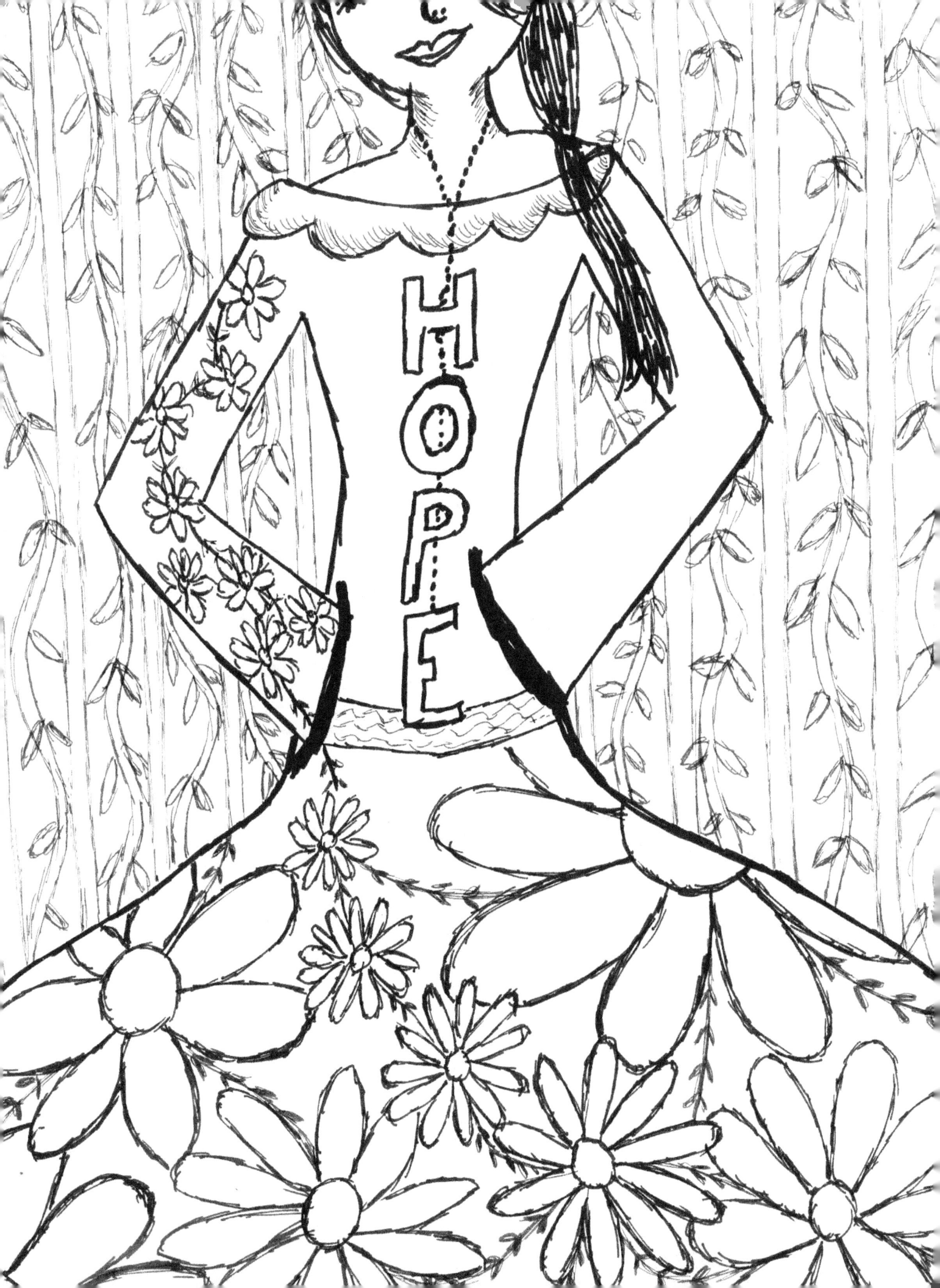

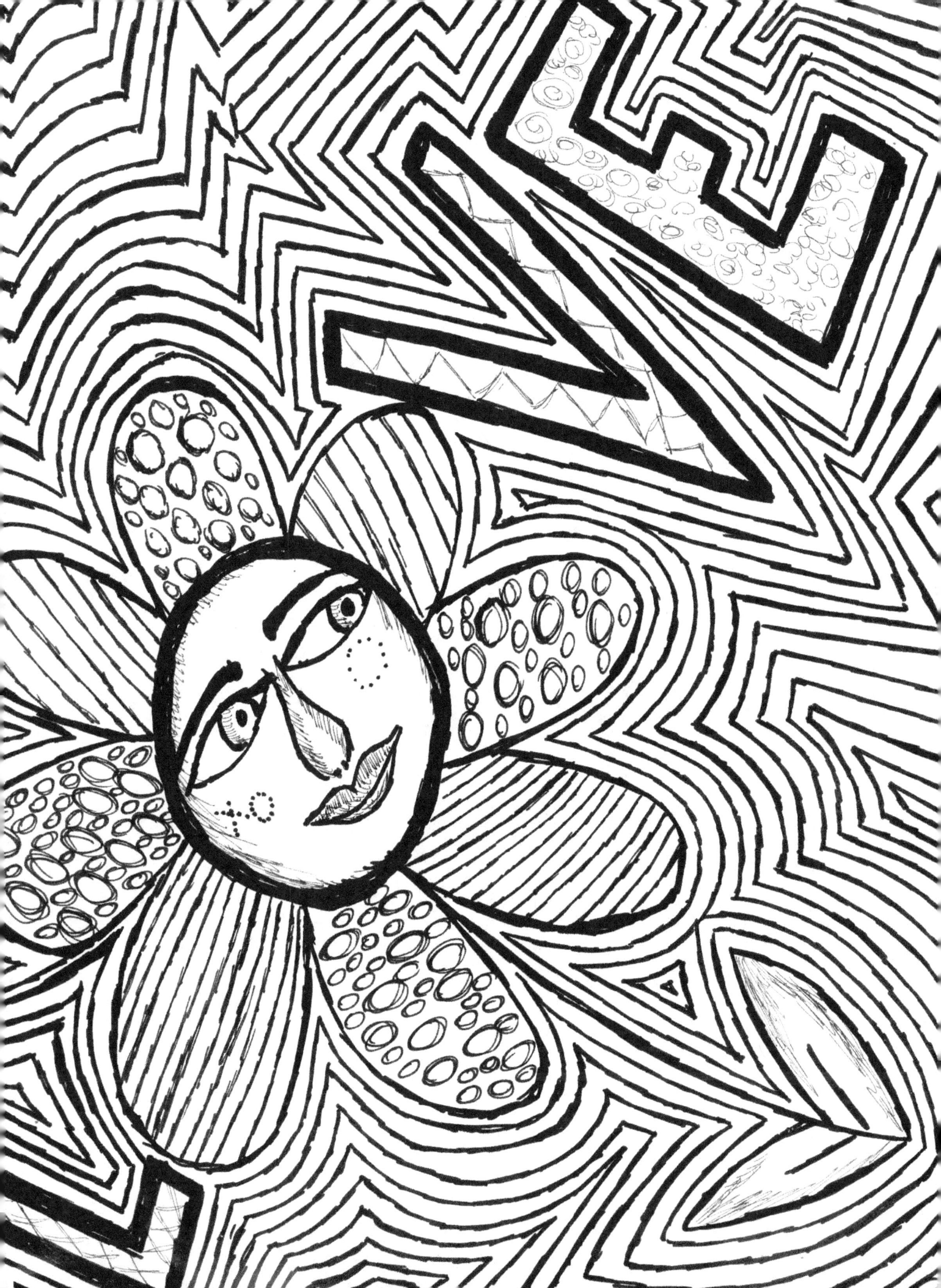

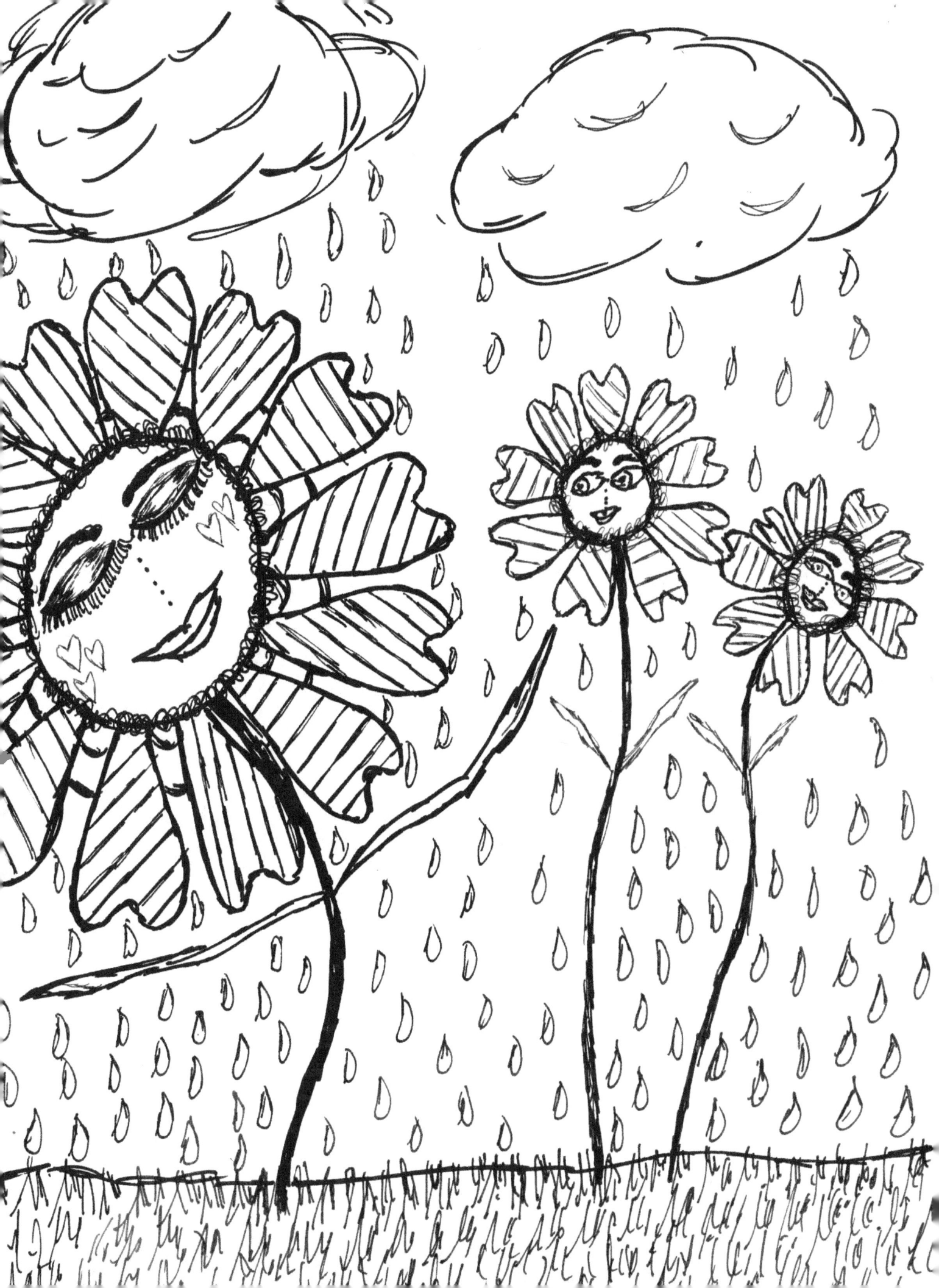

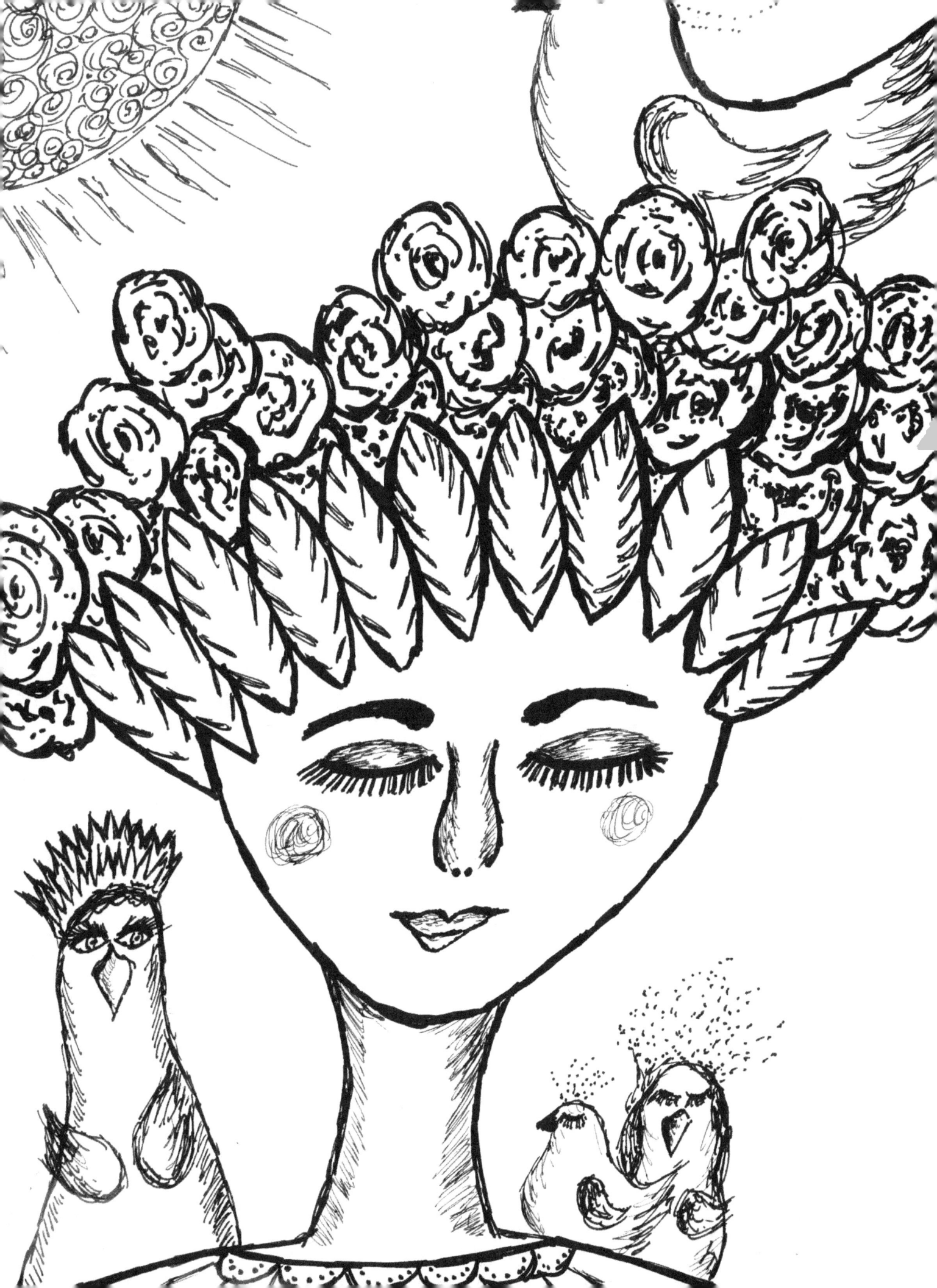

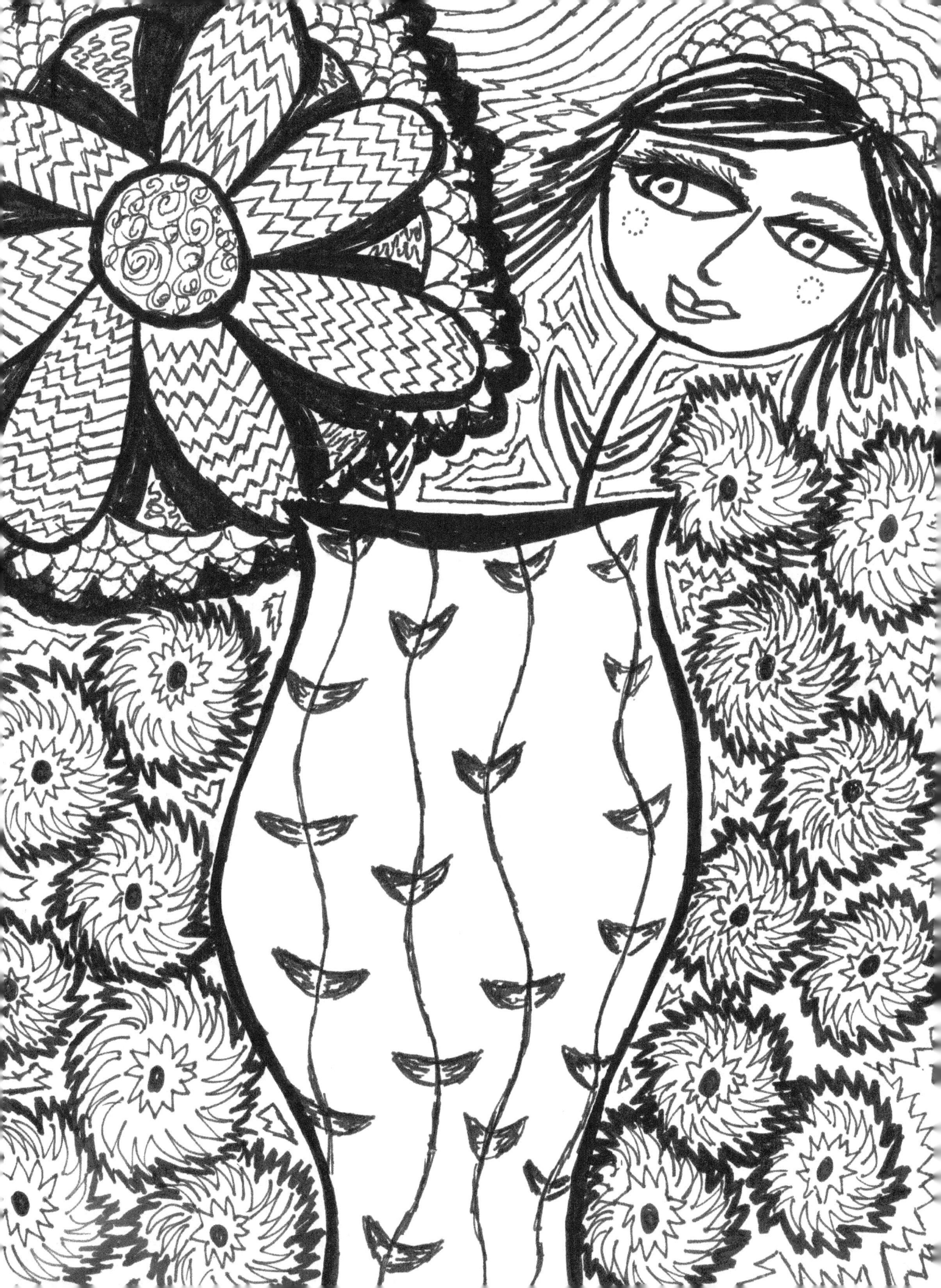

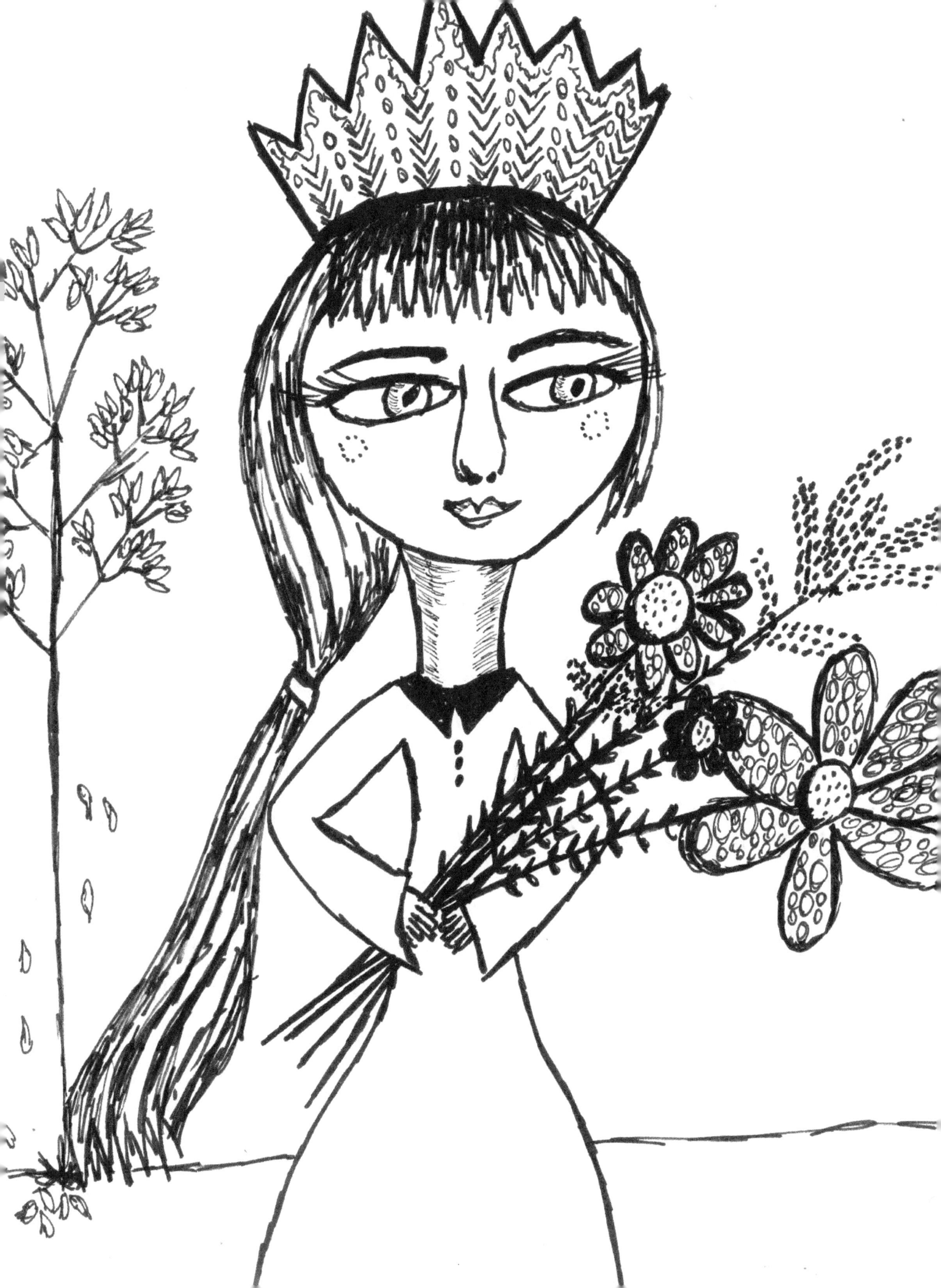

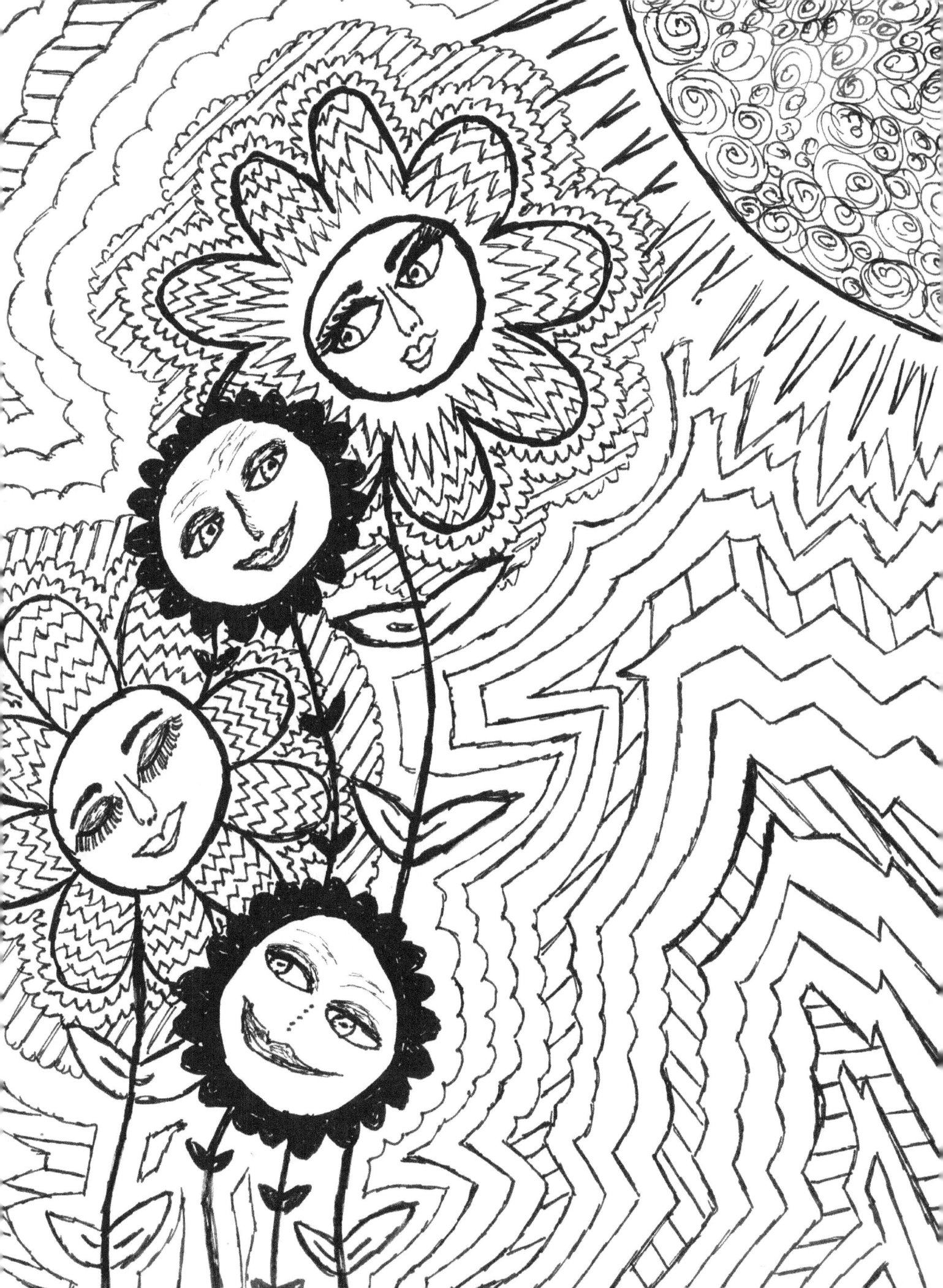

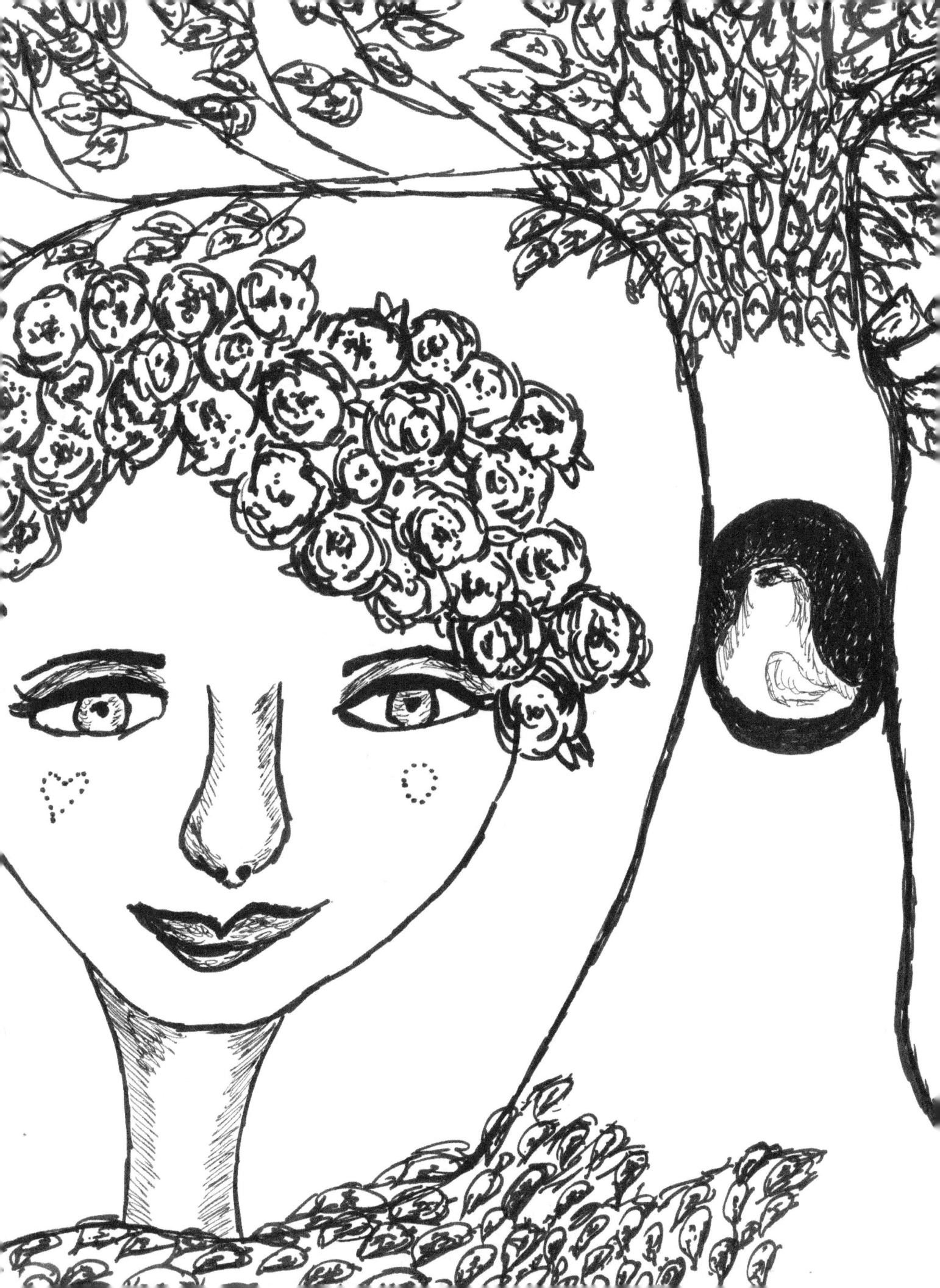

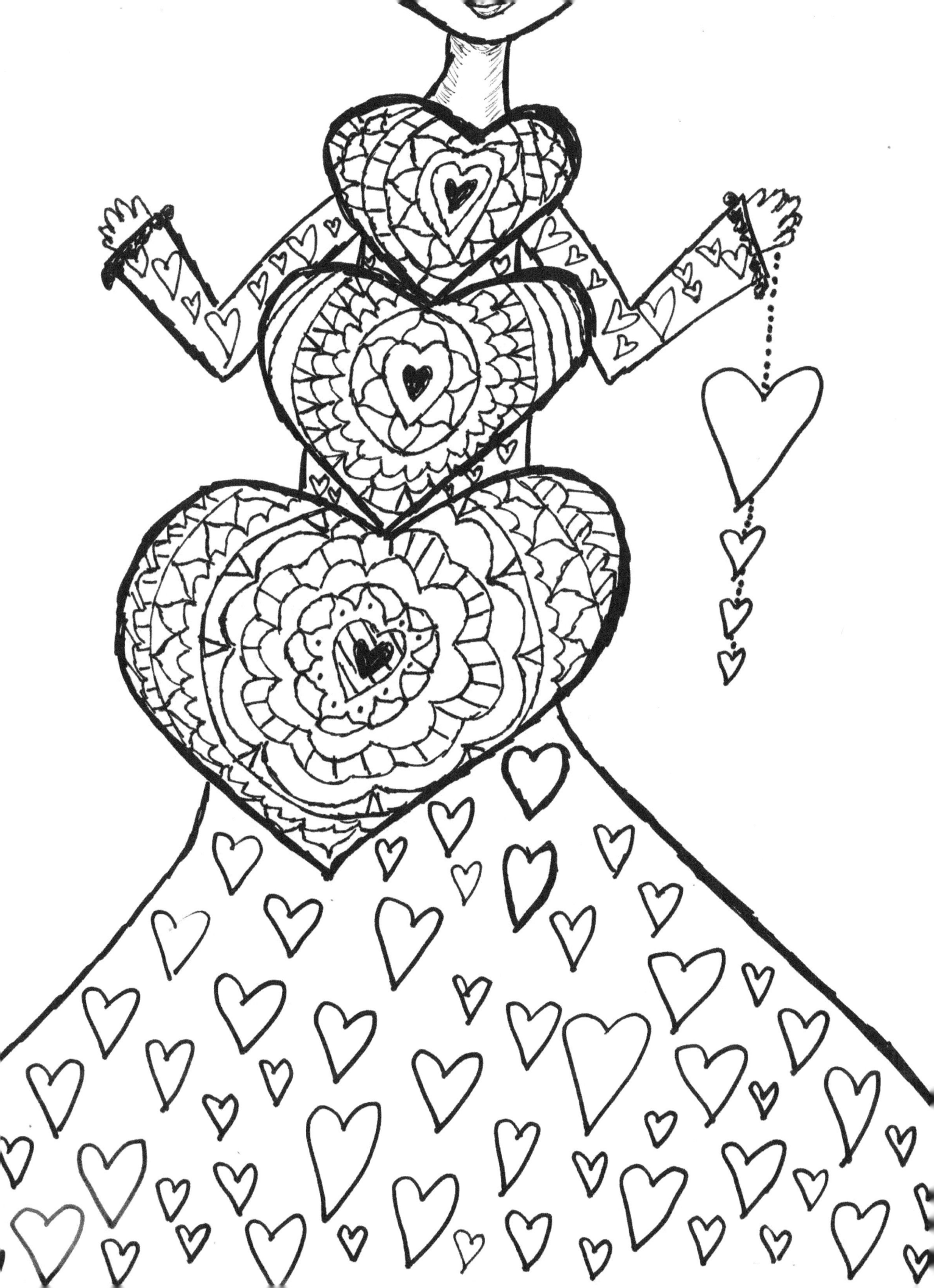

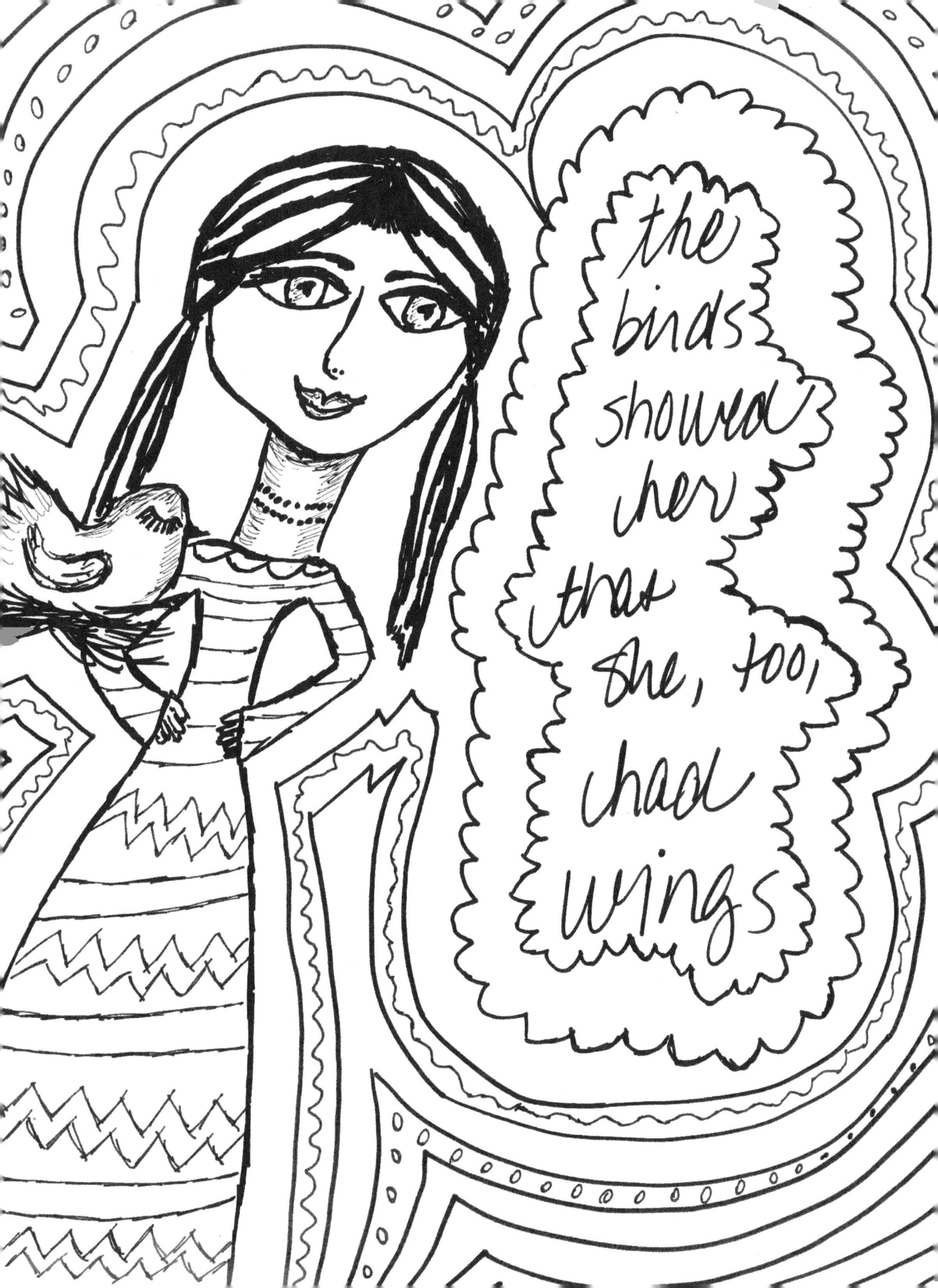

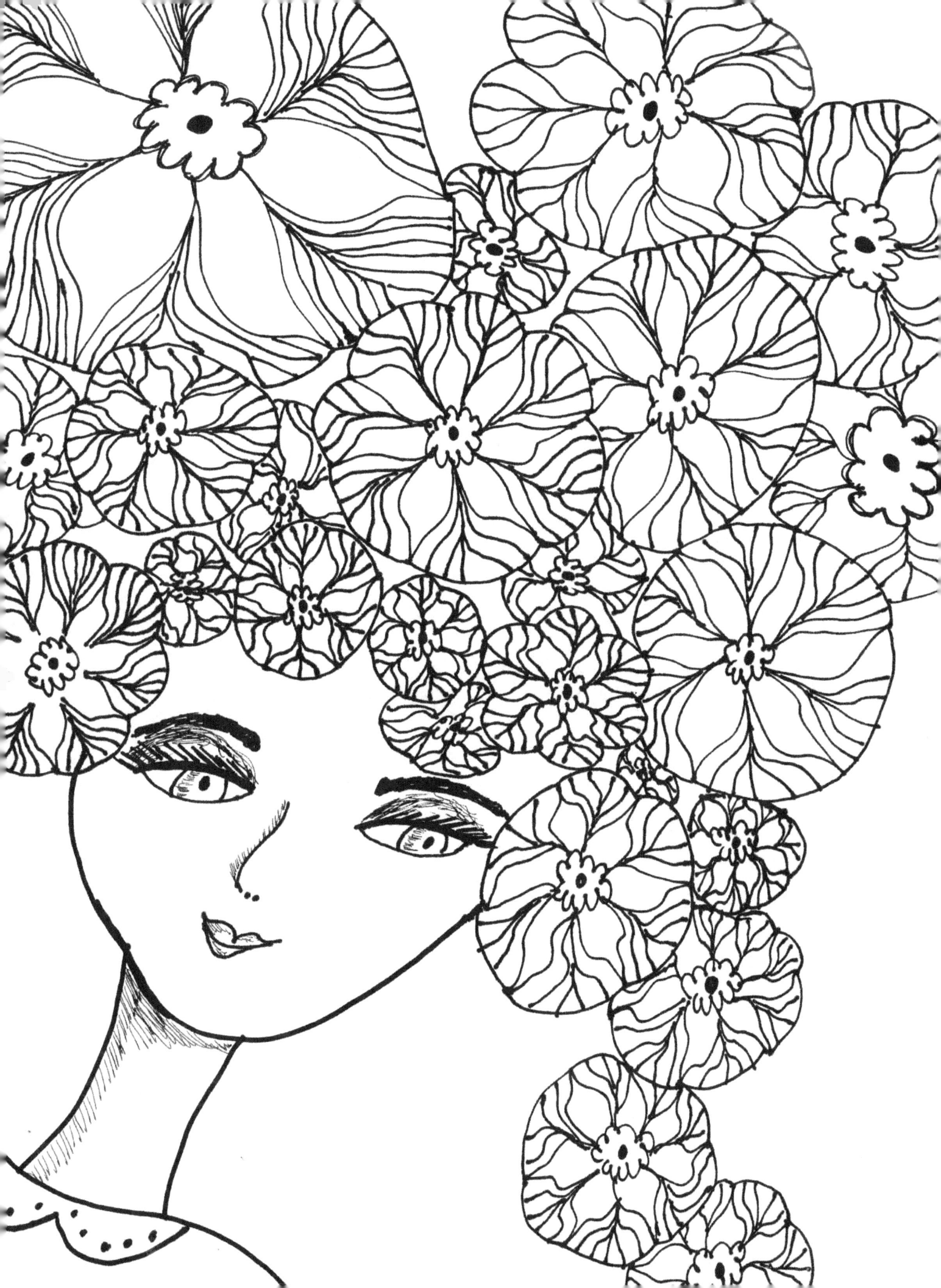

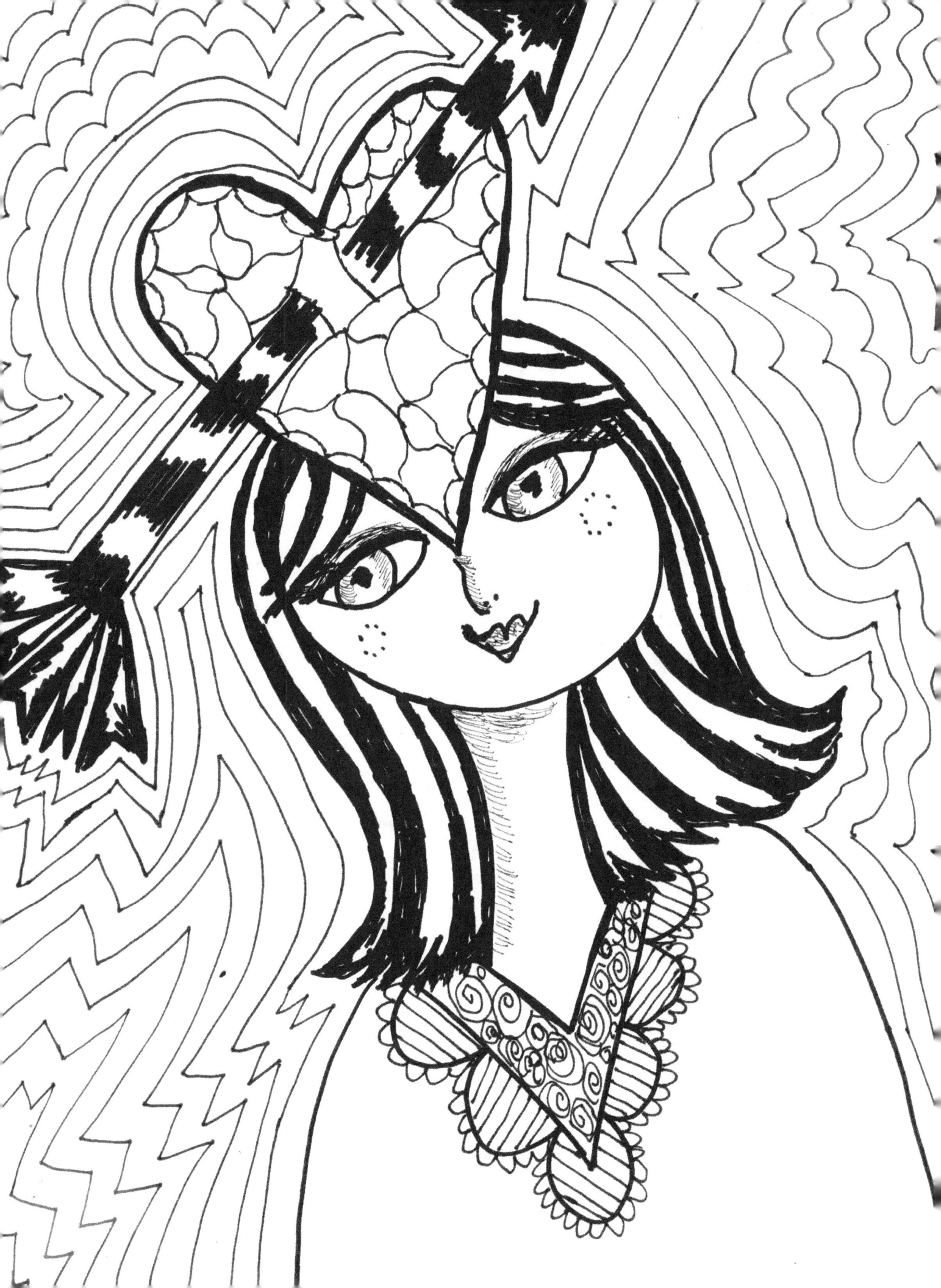

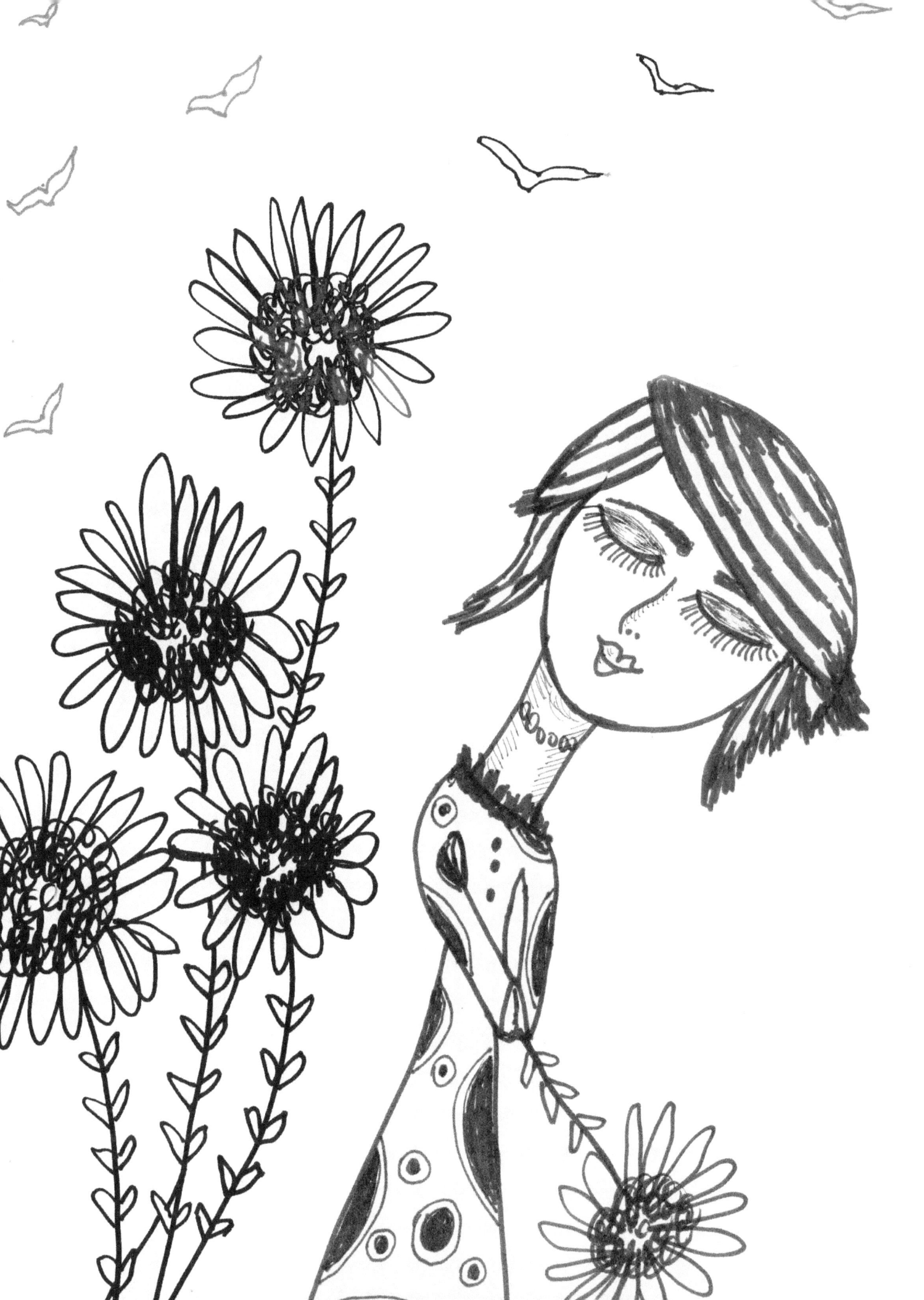

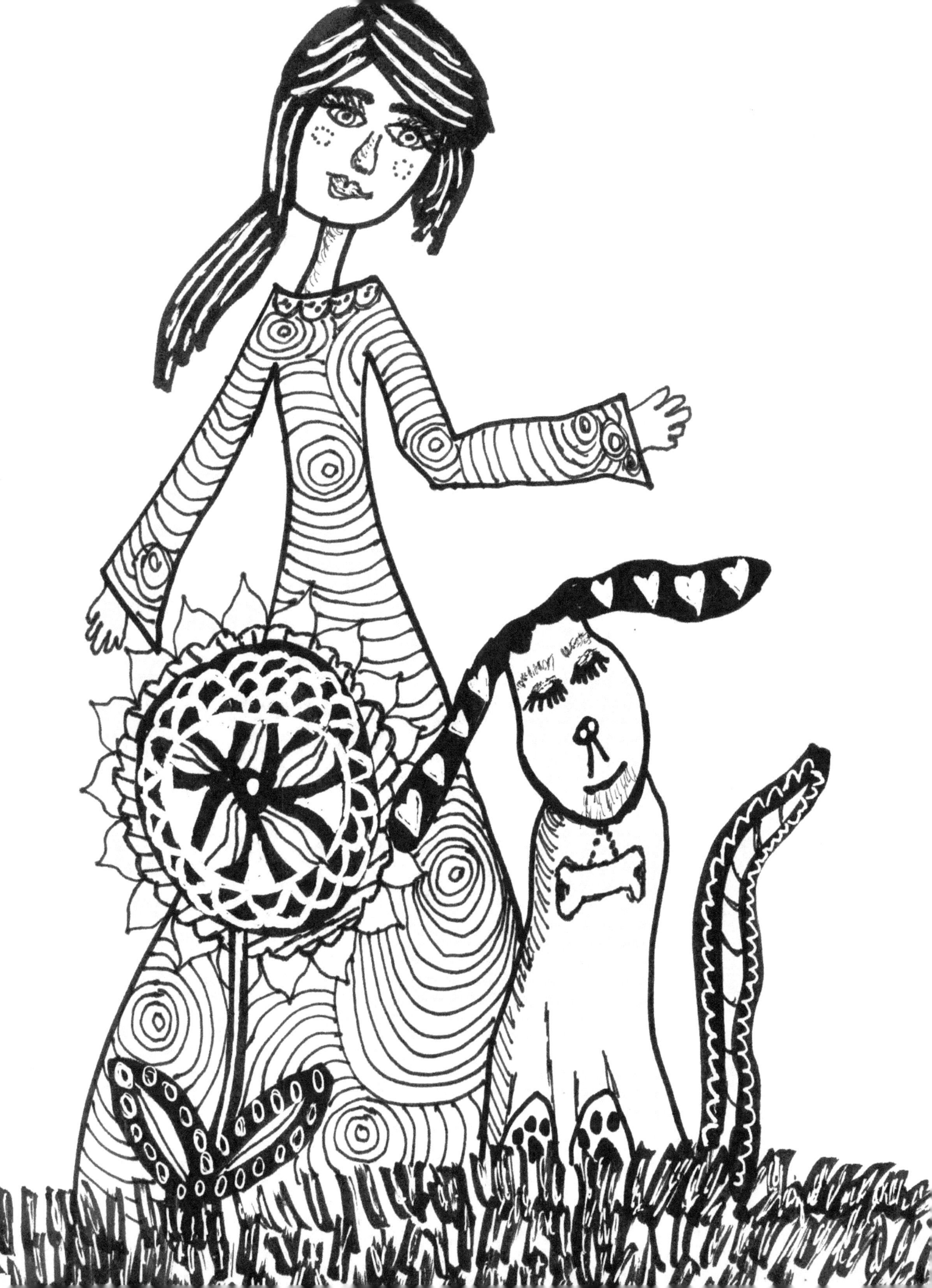

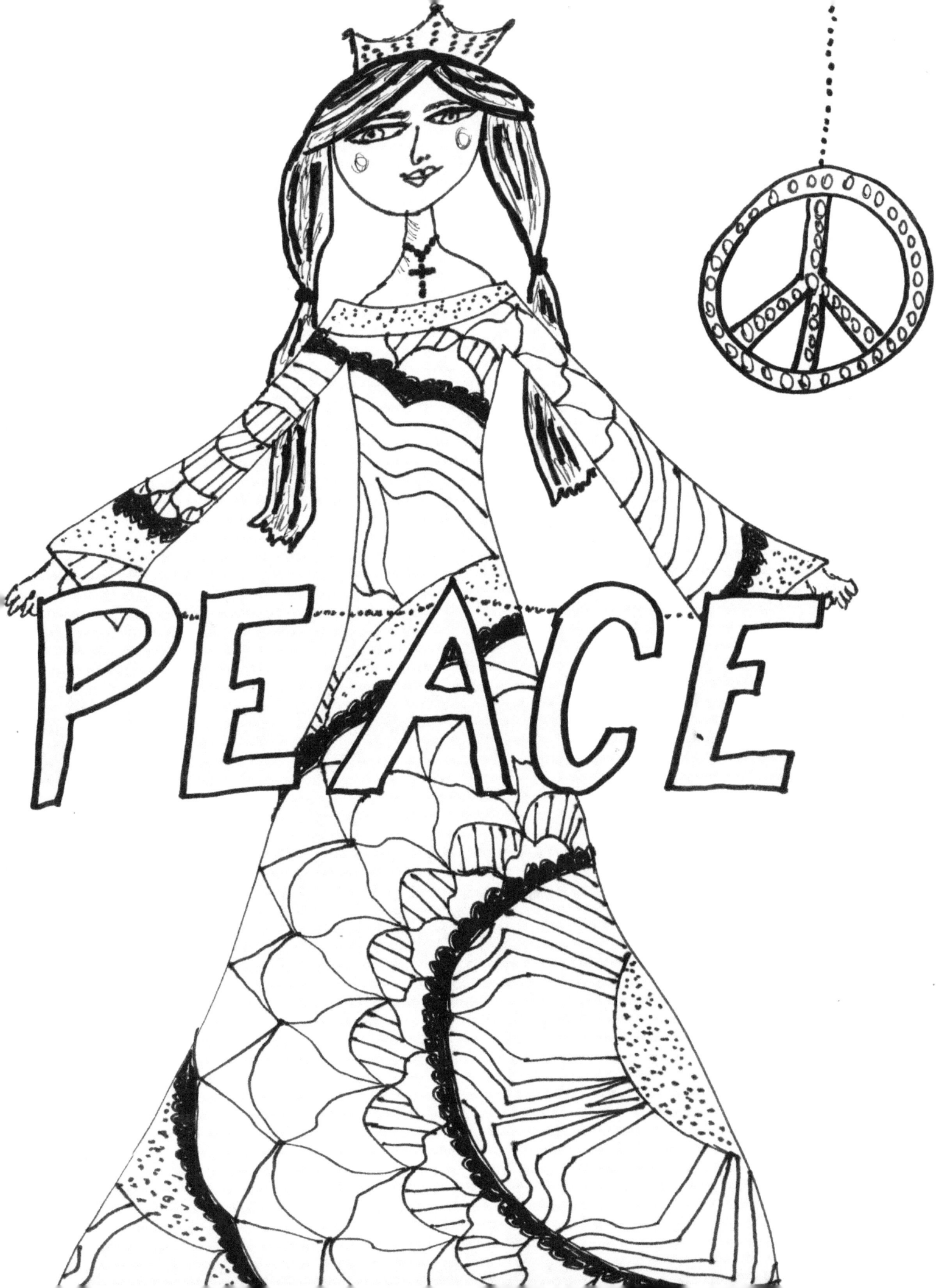

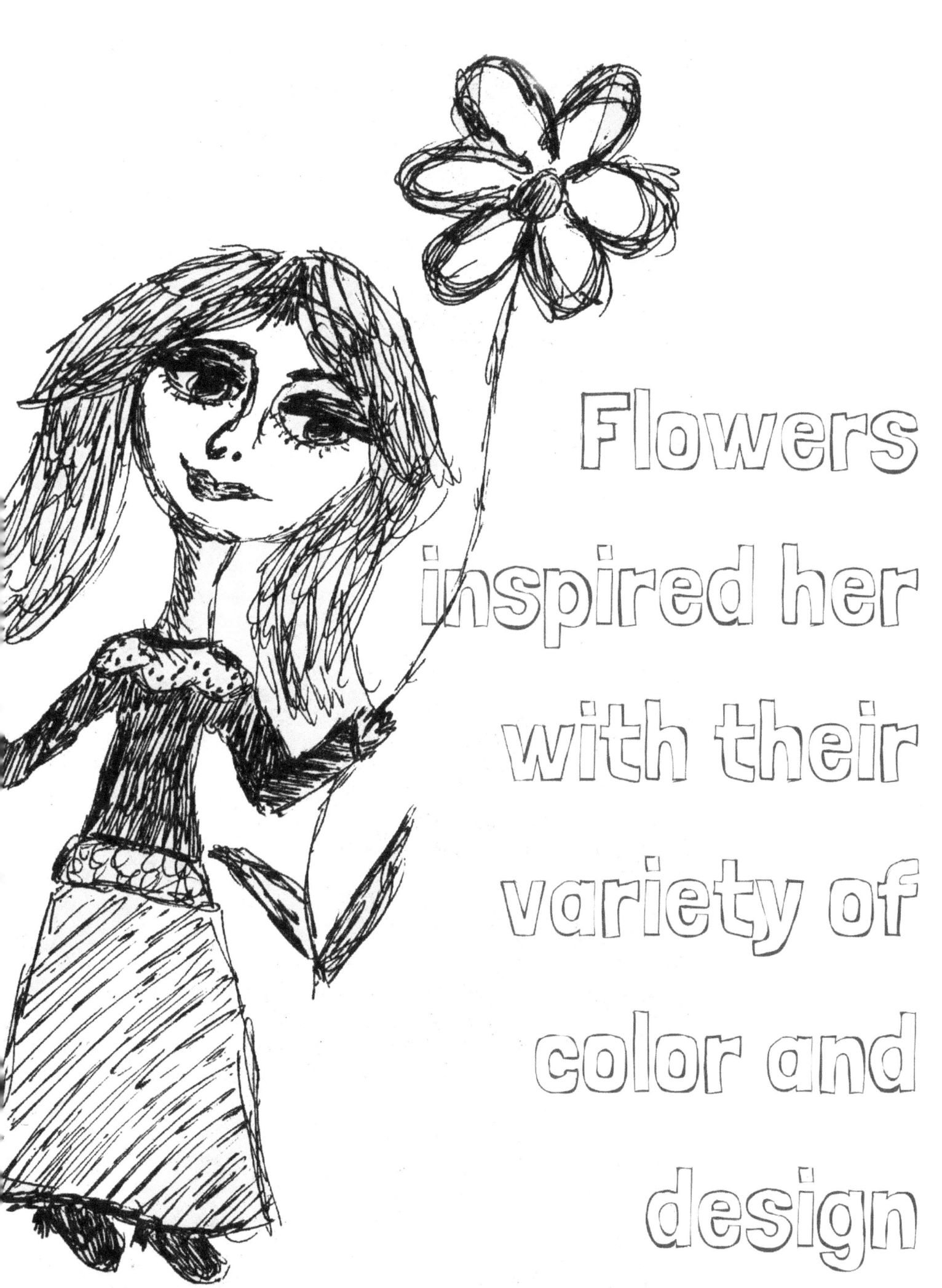

Flowers inspired her with their variety of color and design

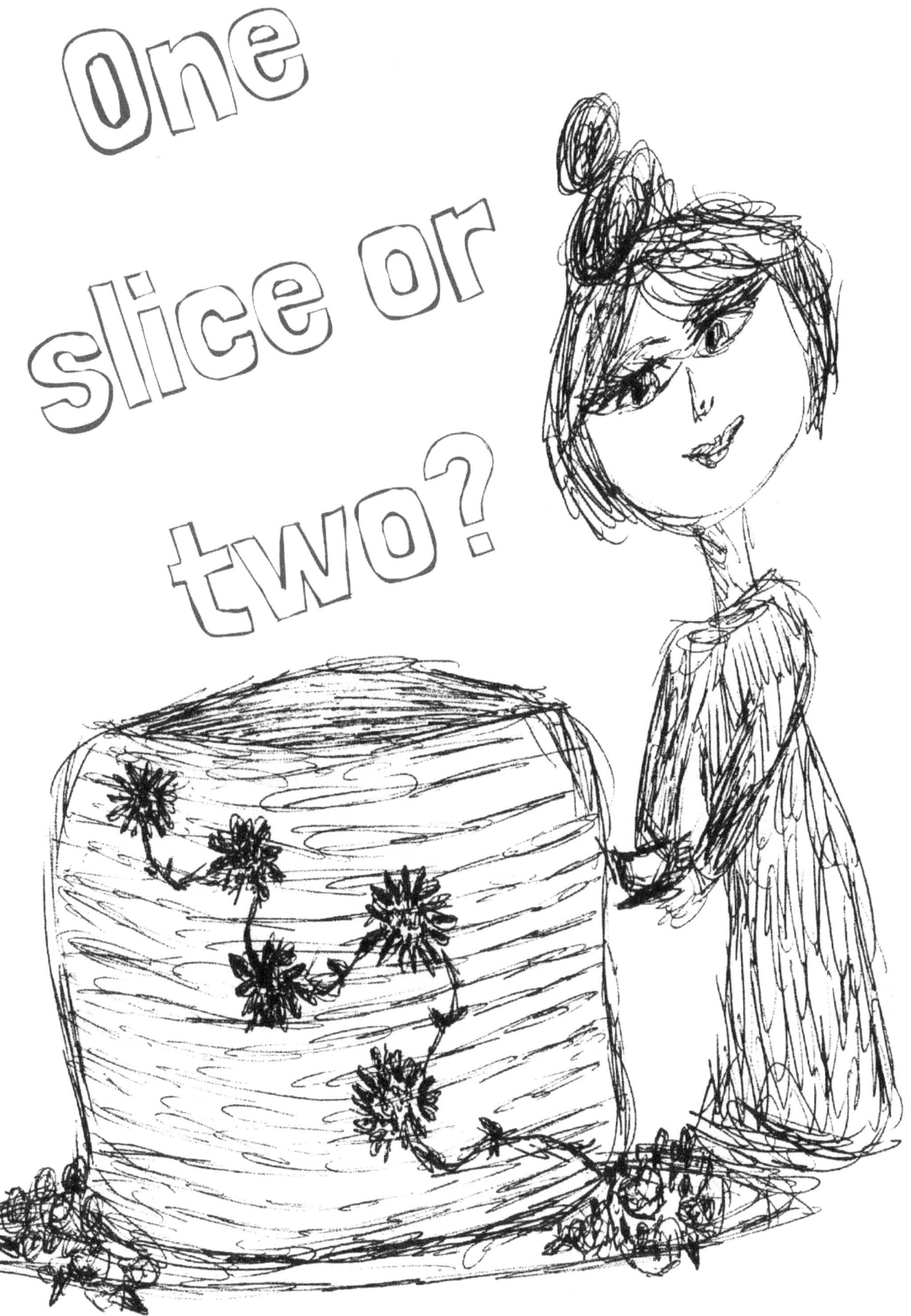

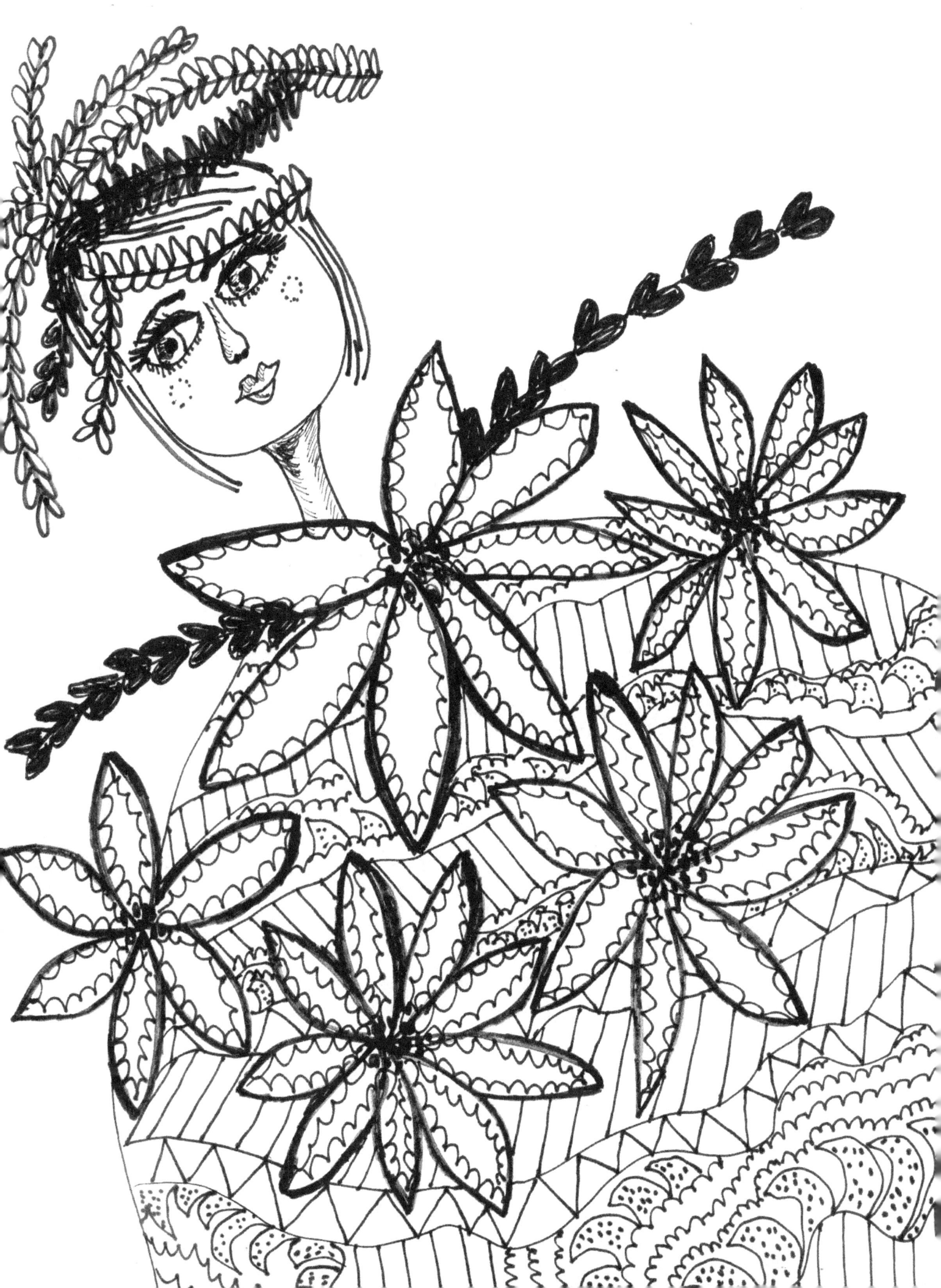

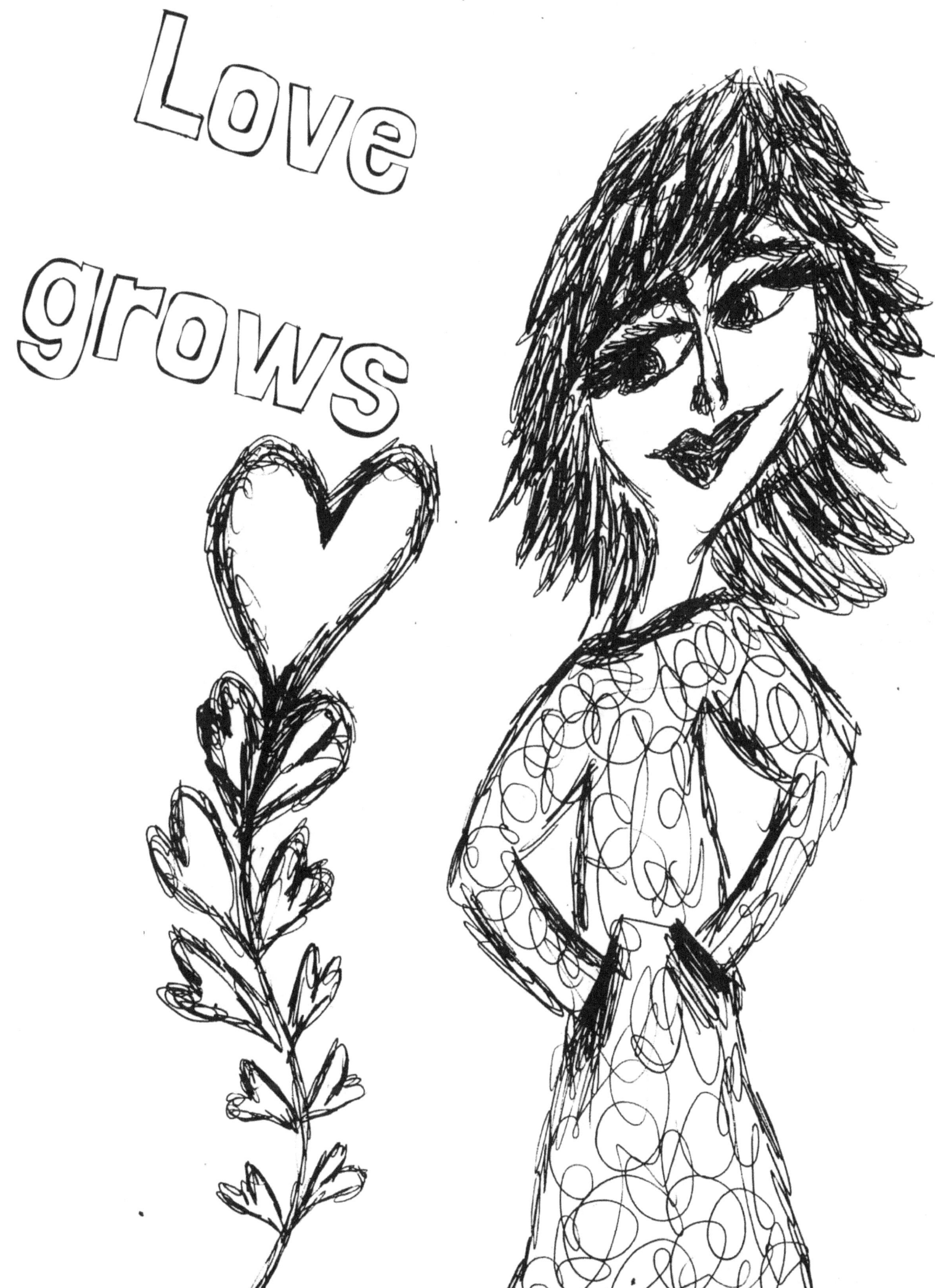

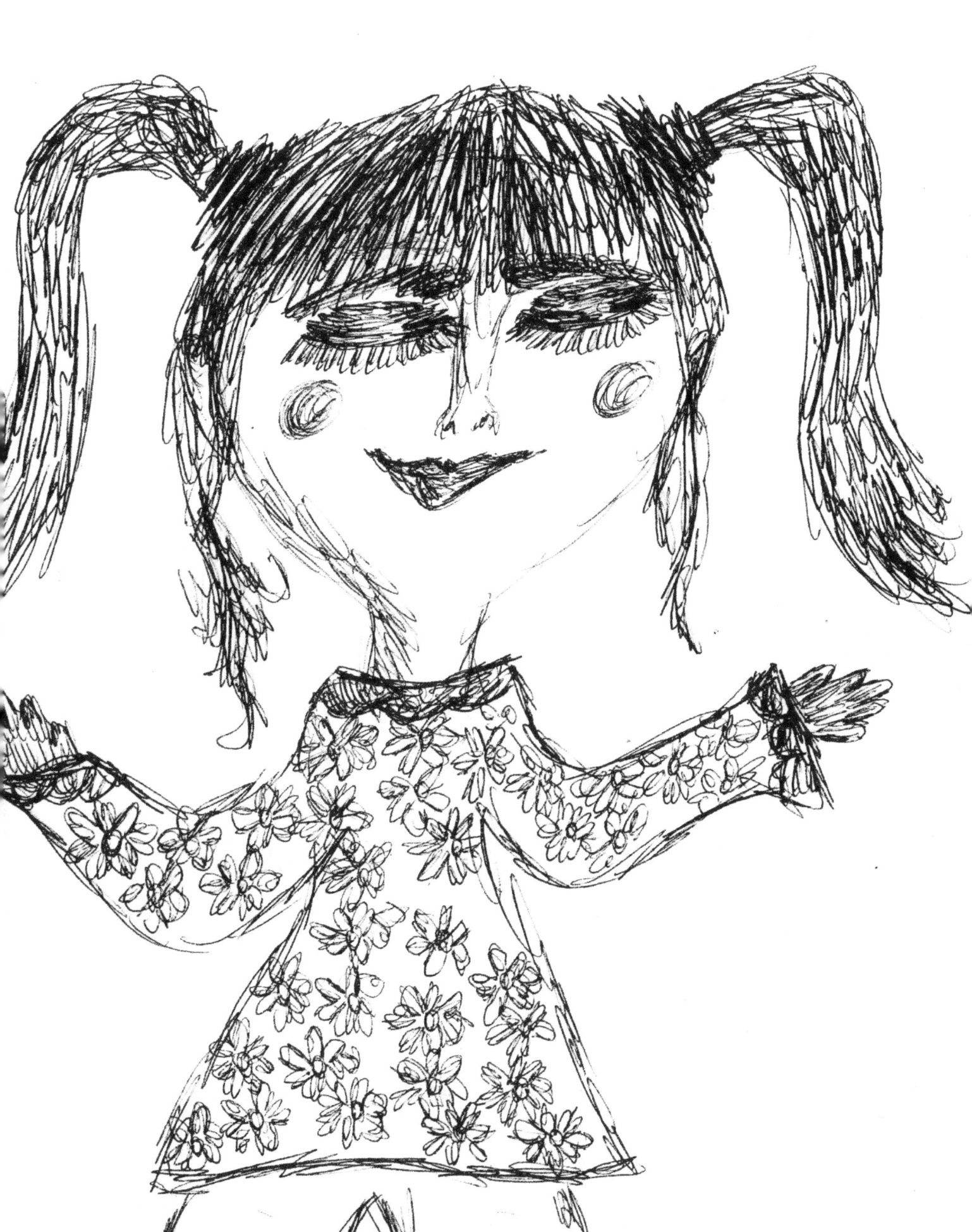

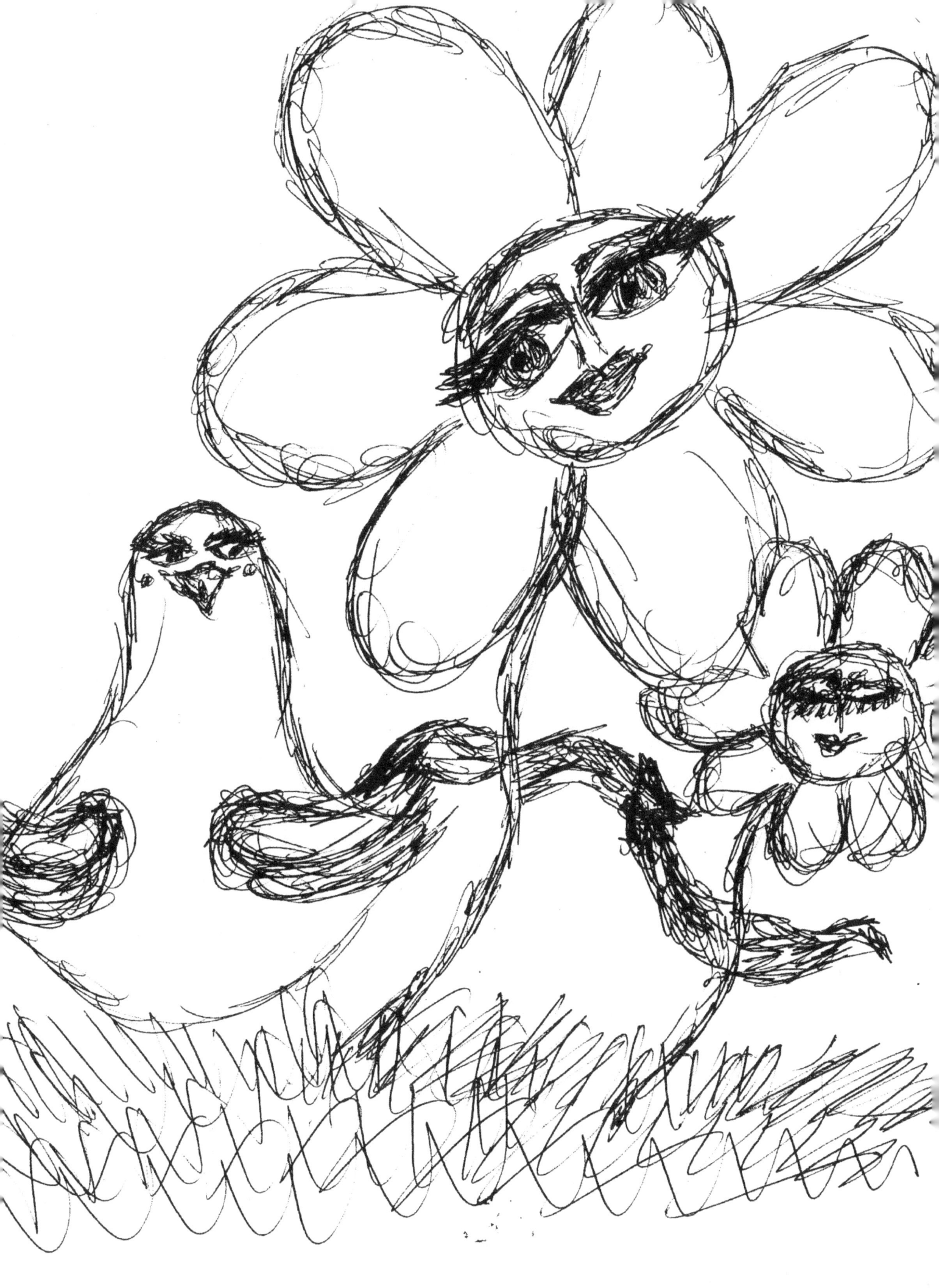

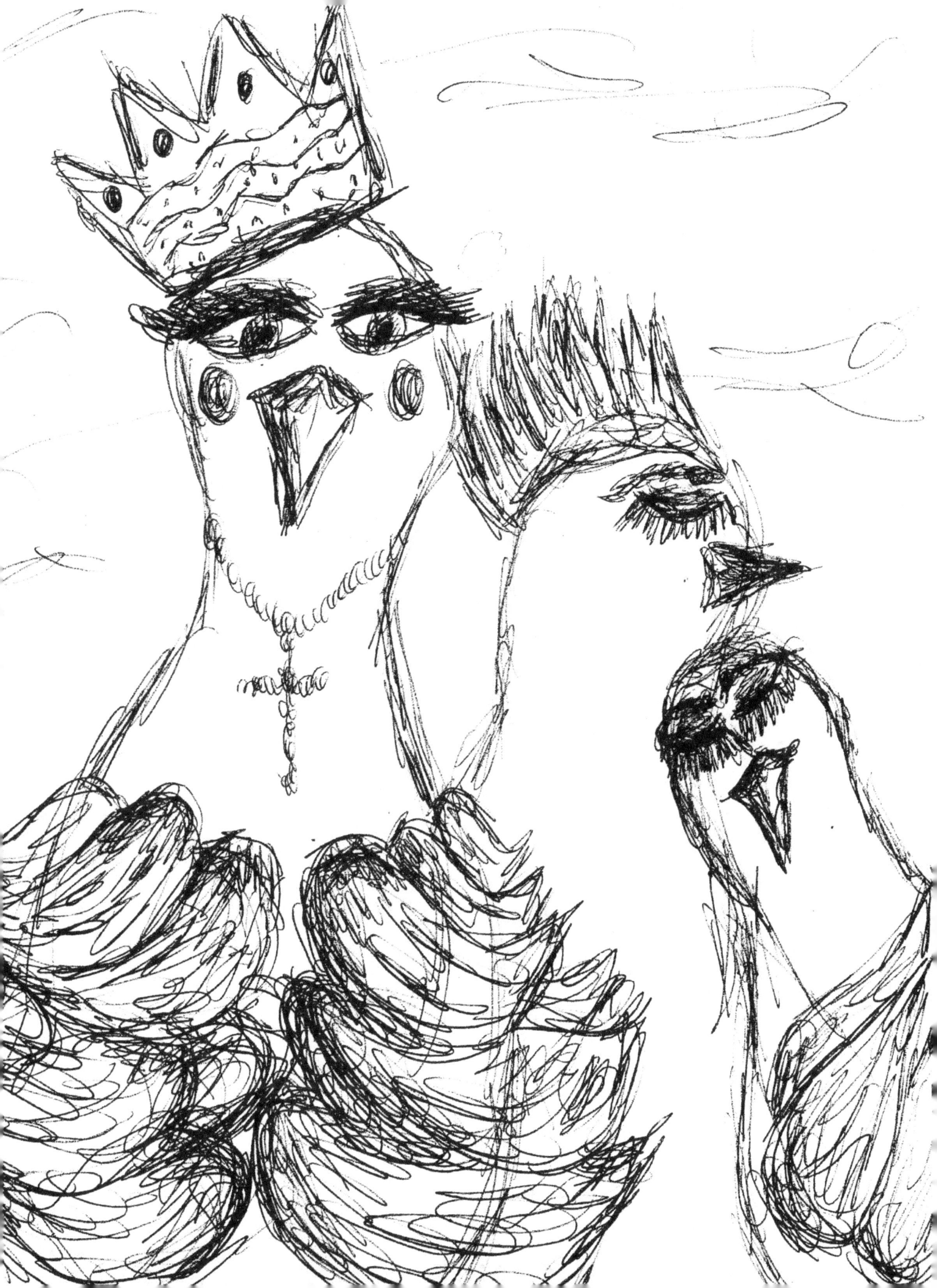

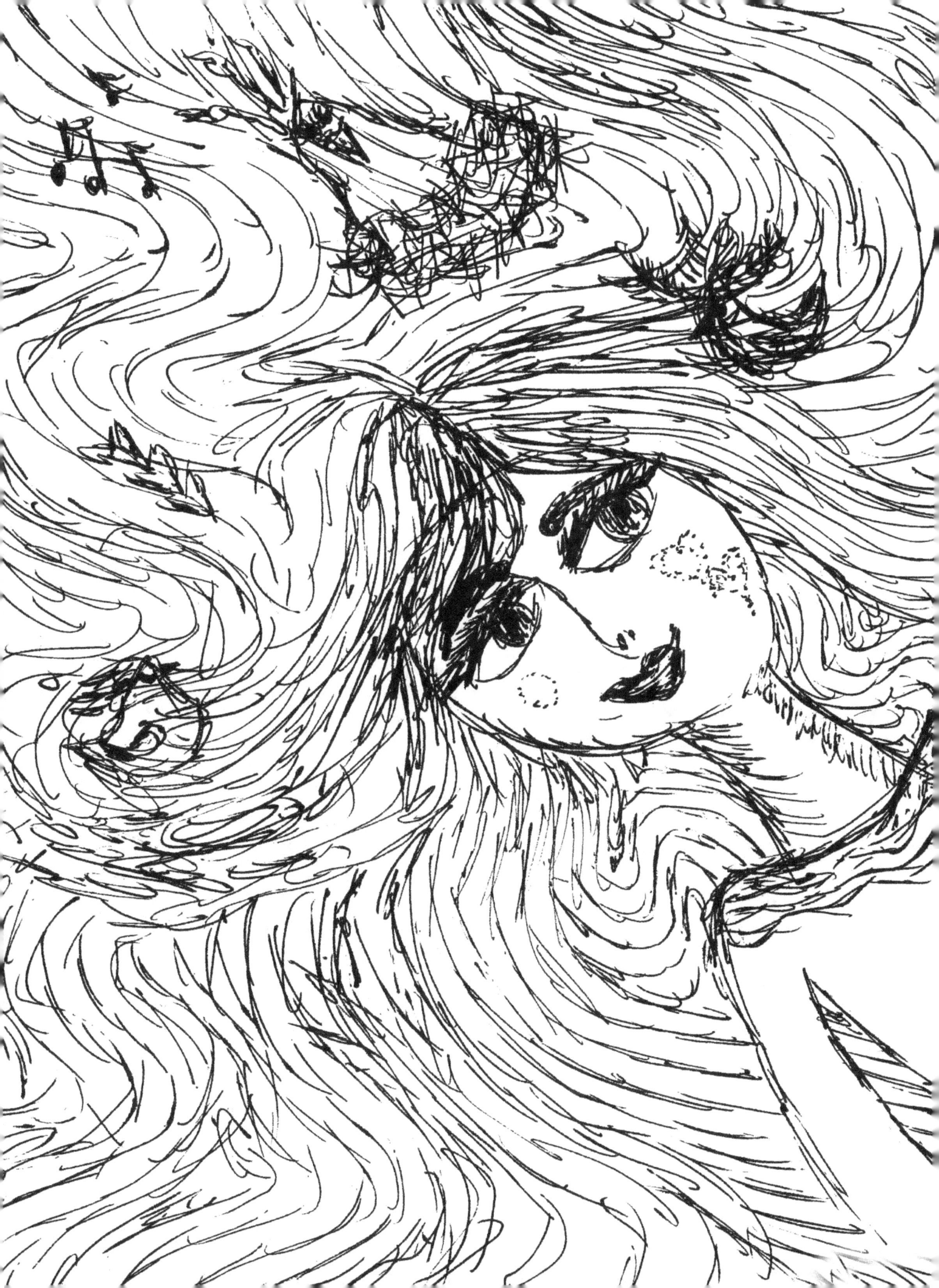

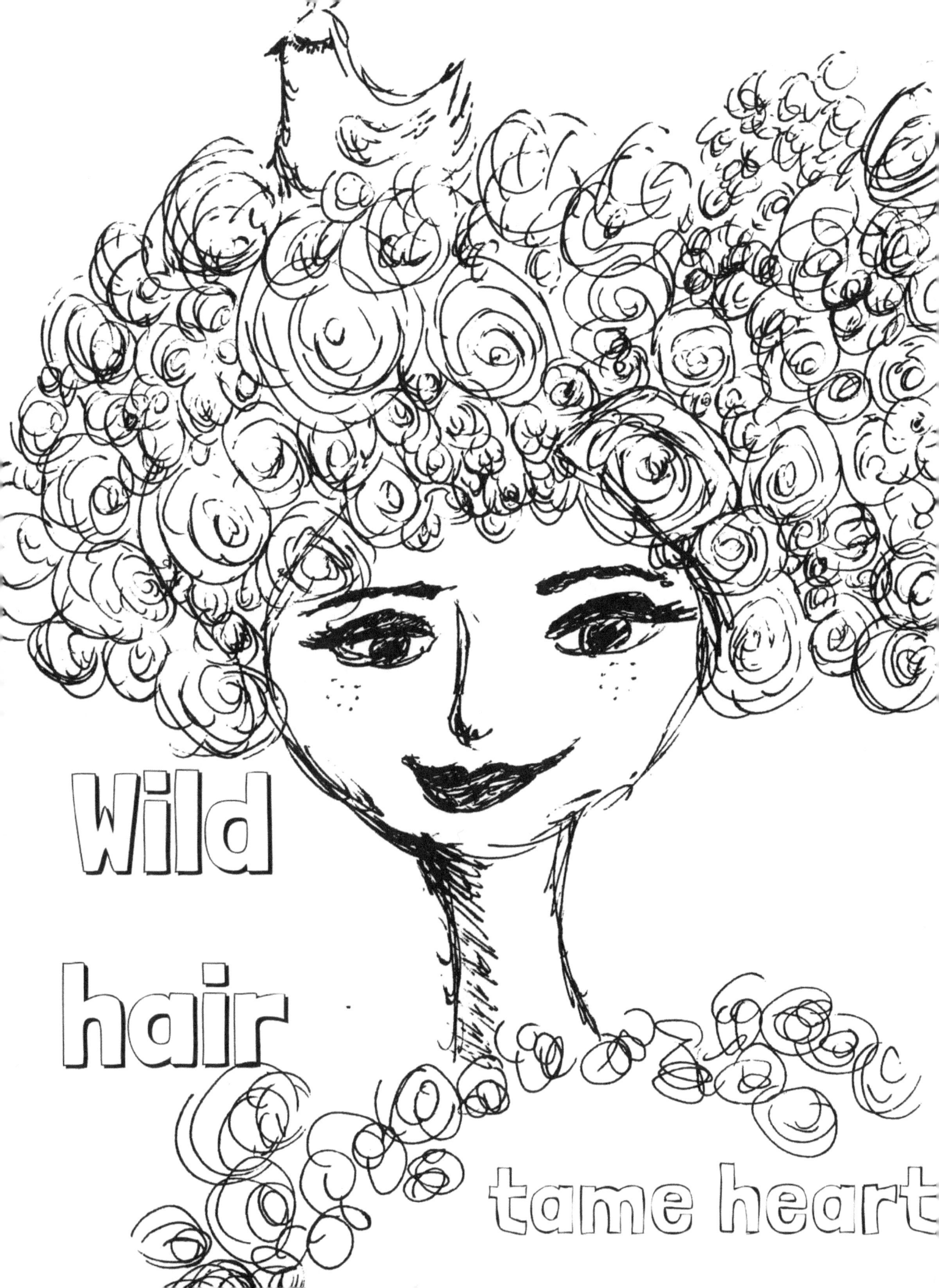

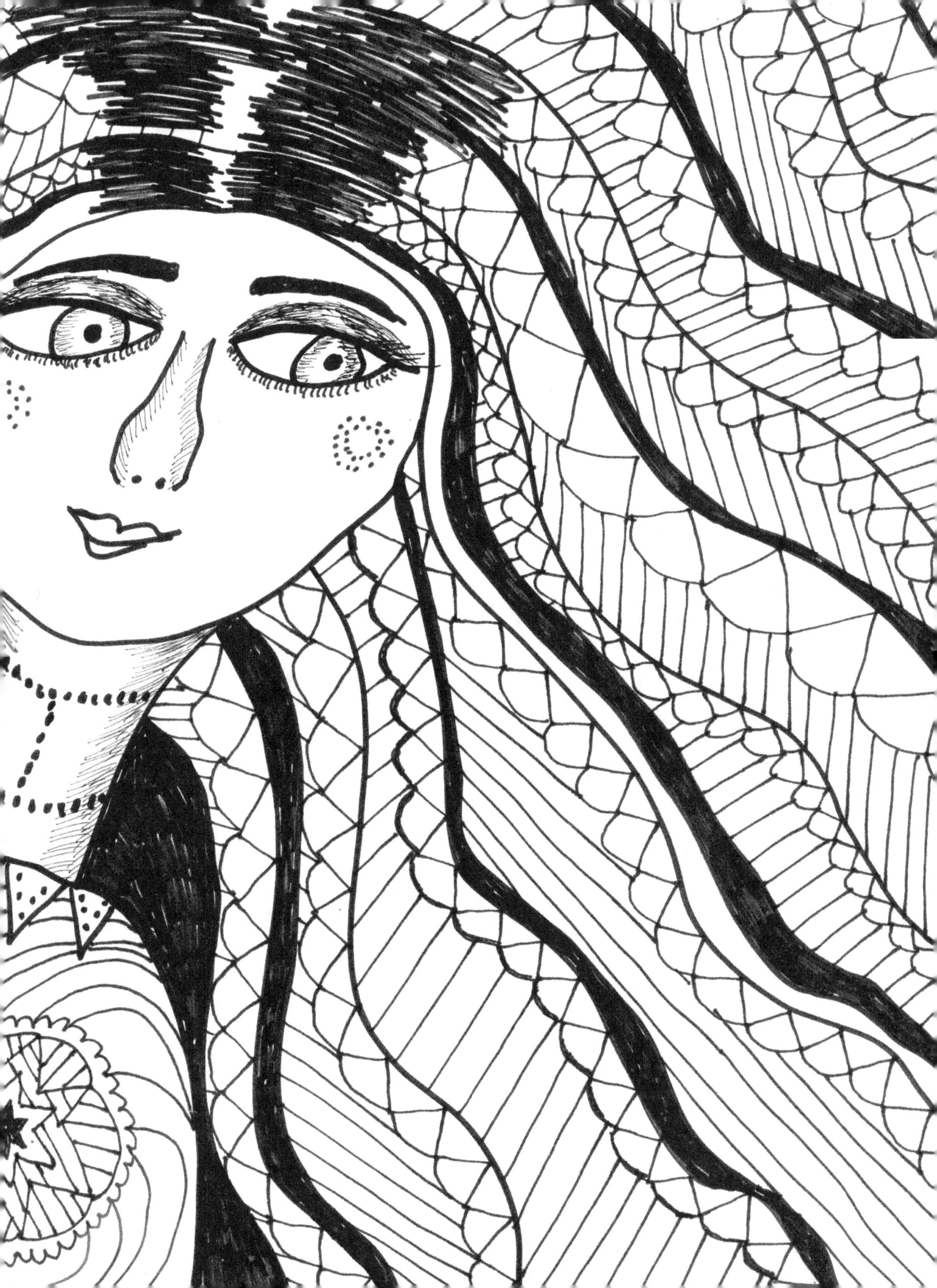

About the Artist

Cherie Burbach is a poet, freelance writer, and mixed media artist.

She paints with a variety of mediums to create art with a hopeful, faith-filled message.

For more on Cherie, visit her website, cherieburbach.com.